MISFITS
A Gothic Fantasy Coloring Book For Adults and Creepy Children

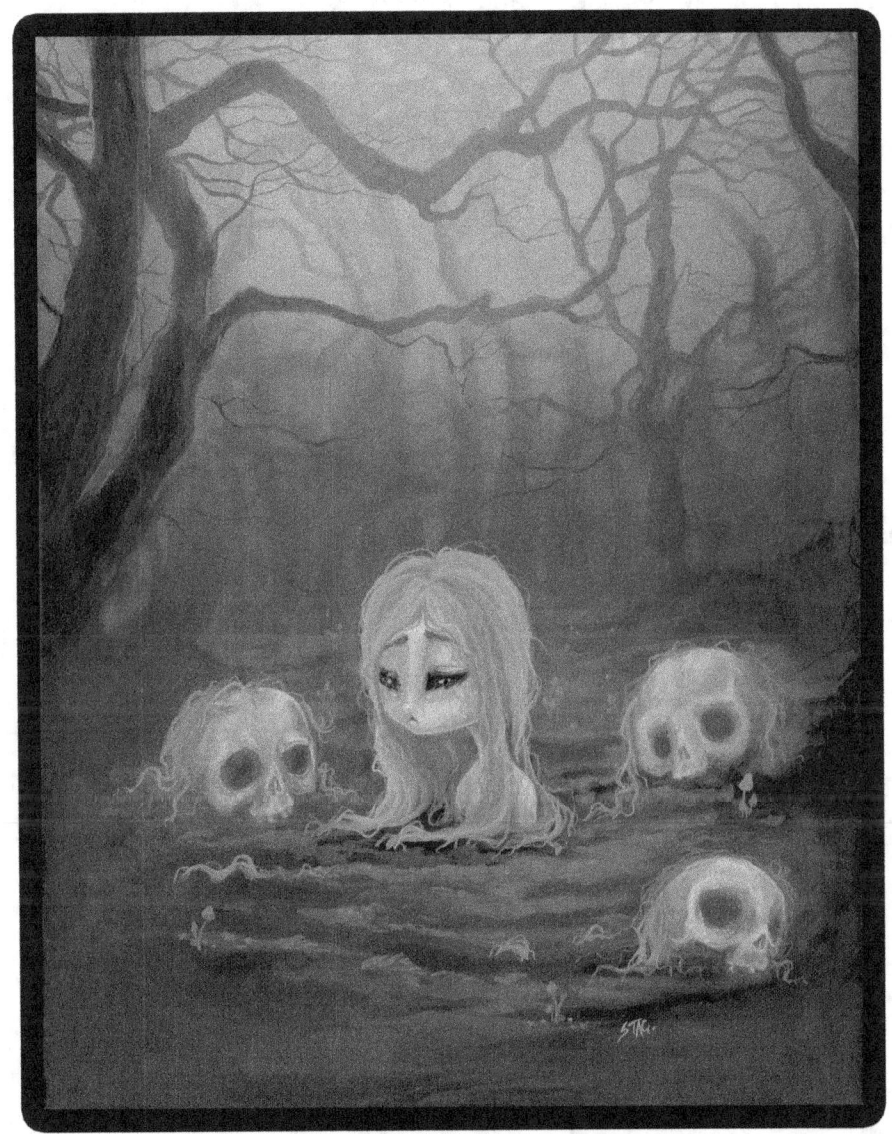

Art by White Stag.
No. 9

25 Gothic fantasy images to color featuring, Vampires, Gloom, Doom, Dead STUFF, Goth fashion, Ghosts and other things Spooky. Art by White Stag is adored by both young and old for its whimsical, creepy and cute depictions of sometimes dark and sometimes sweet little girls and creatures.

ISBN - 978-1978181786

All Artwork copyright 2017 White Stag, All Rights Reserved (Terra Bidlespacher). Misfits A Coloring Book for Adults and Odd Children Vol. 8
First Edition published 2017. No part of this book may be reproduced, edited or redistributed without consent.

Helpful Tips

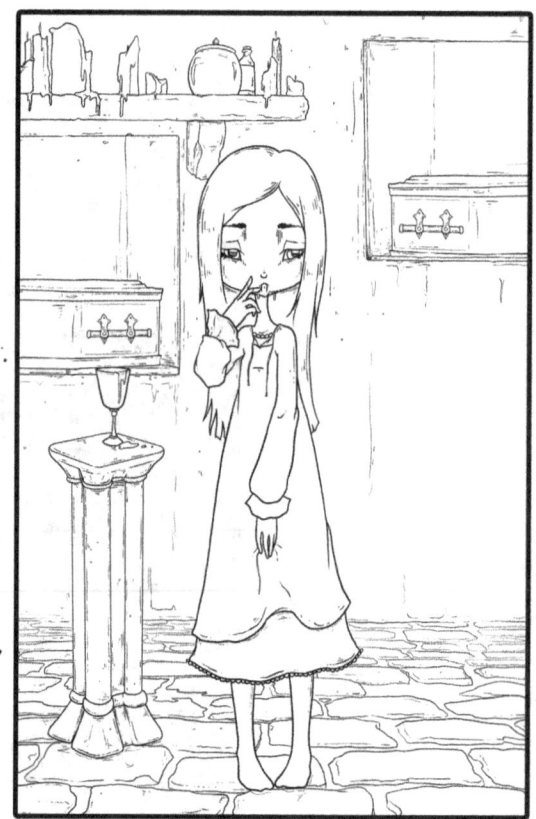

★ When coloring always use clean sheets of paper between the back of the page you are working on and the rest of the pages of the book. It will help to avoid bleed through or indentions on other pages by accident.

★ It doesn't hurt to have a test sheet for testing color schemes too. Sometimes colors may seem like they will look good side by side but seeing them first definitely helps.

★ Always test pens and markers before using. You might find clogged or dried markers/pens can quickly ruin an image you are coloring and could make it near impossible to fix.

★ Make sure to keep colored pencils sharp! The sharper the better.

★ Don't forget to take your time, you'll get much better results if you don't rush.

★ Remember, there really is no wrong! HAVE FUN! Spank it with glitter, give it a bow, or ignore the "rules" and color outside of the lines! Who cares, just have fun doing it!

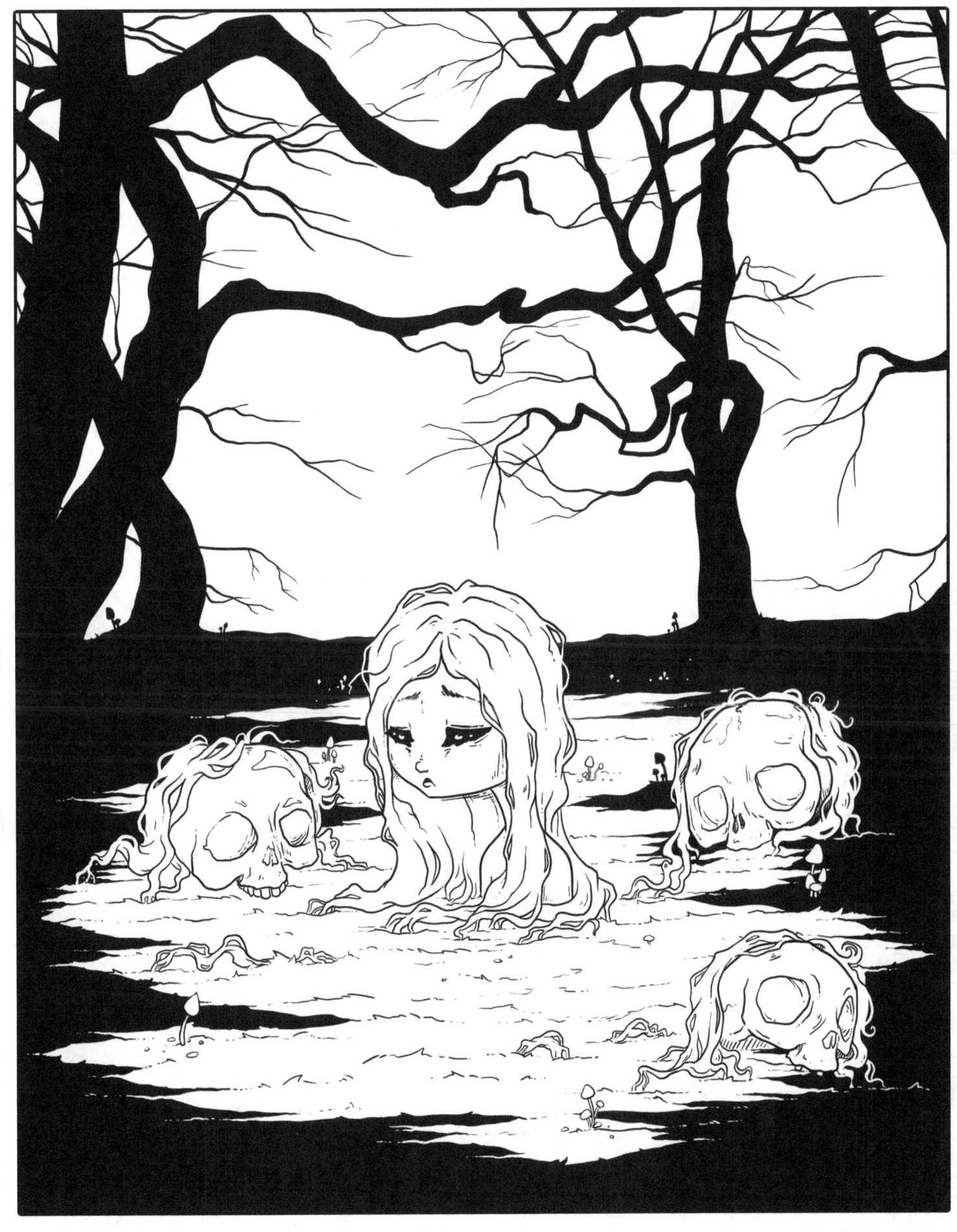

THE HUMAN GARDEN

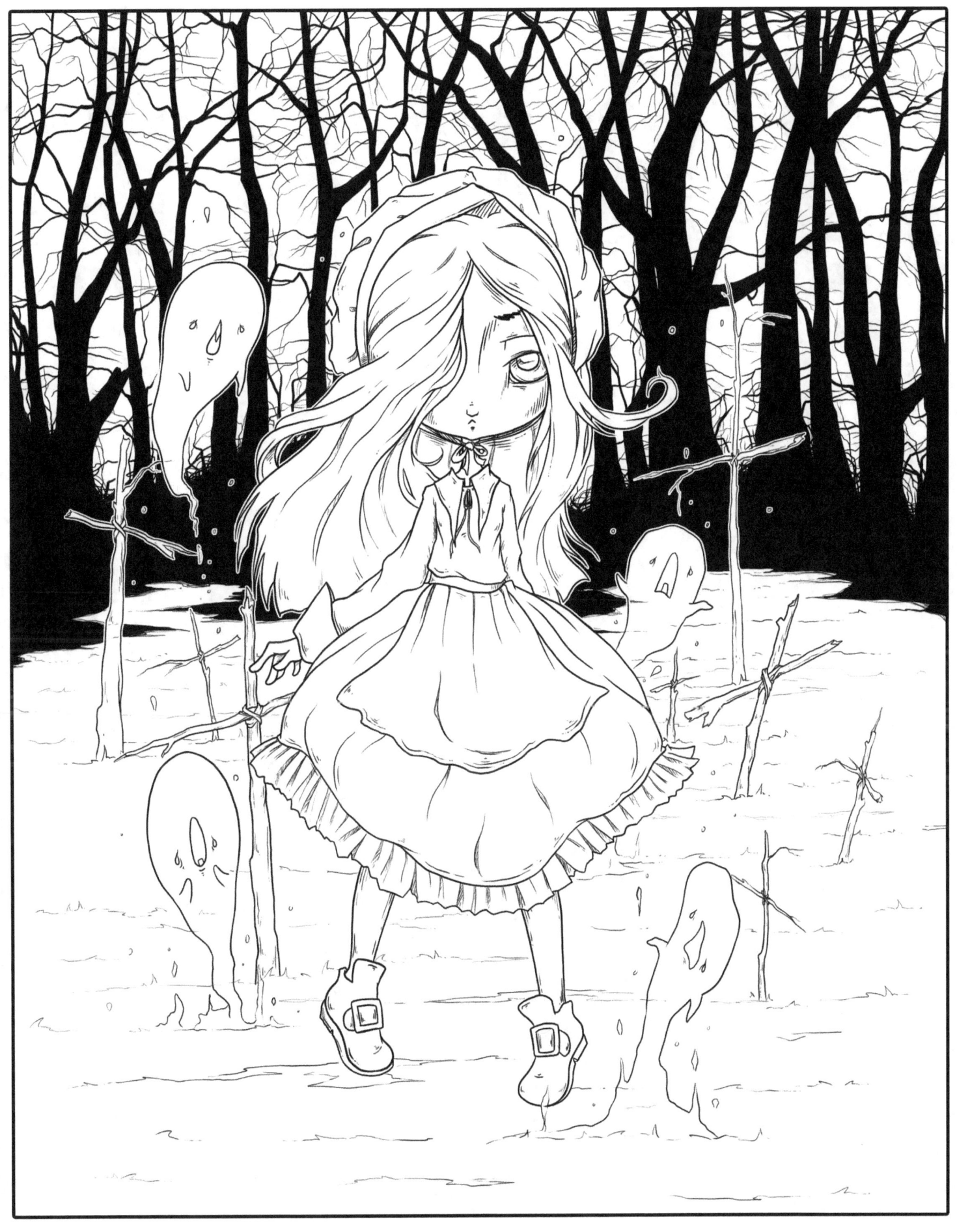

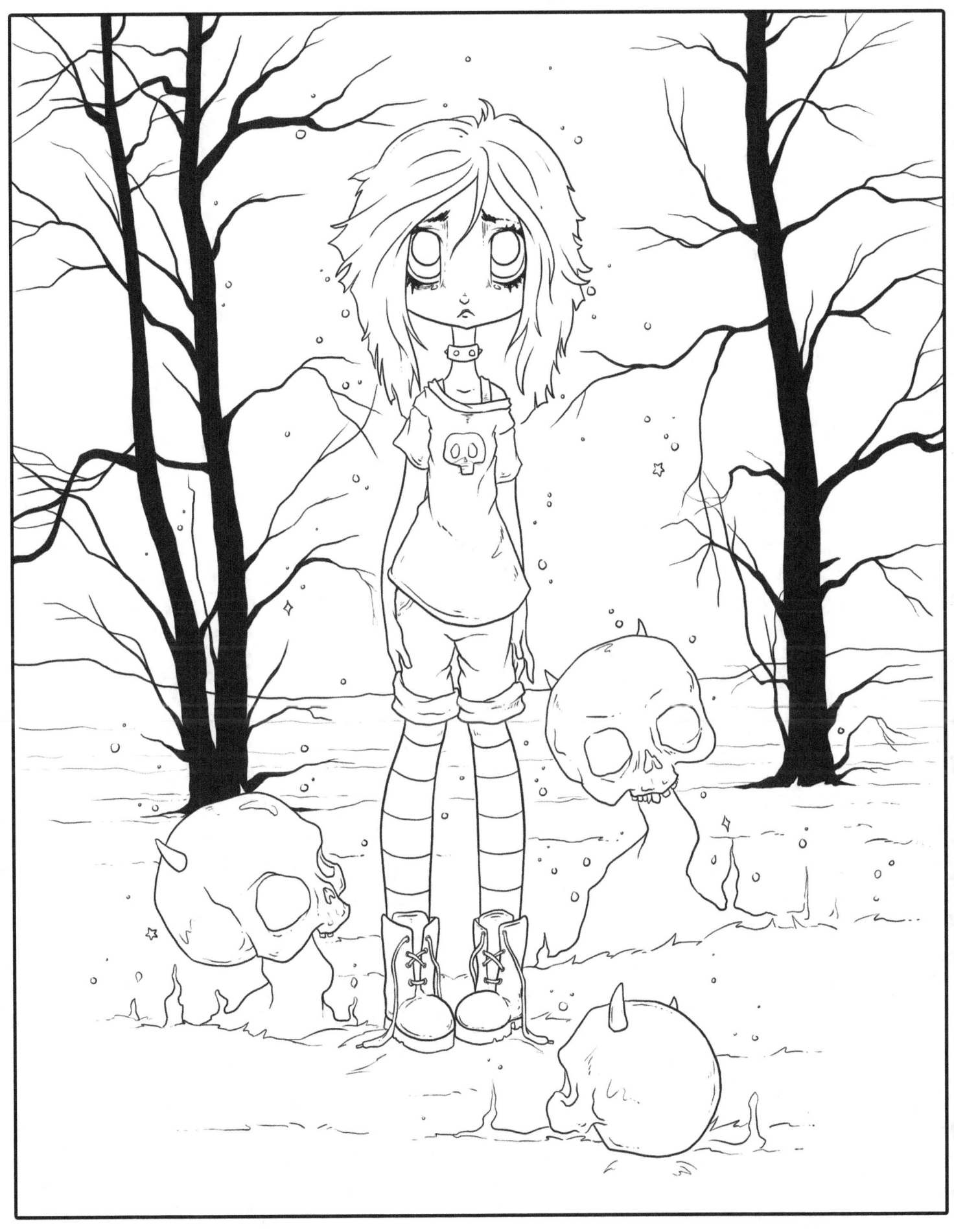

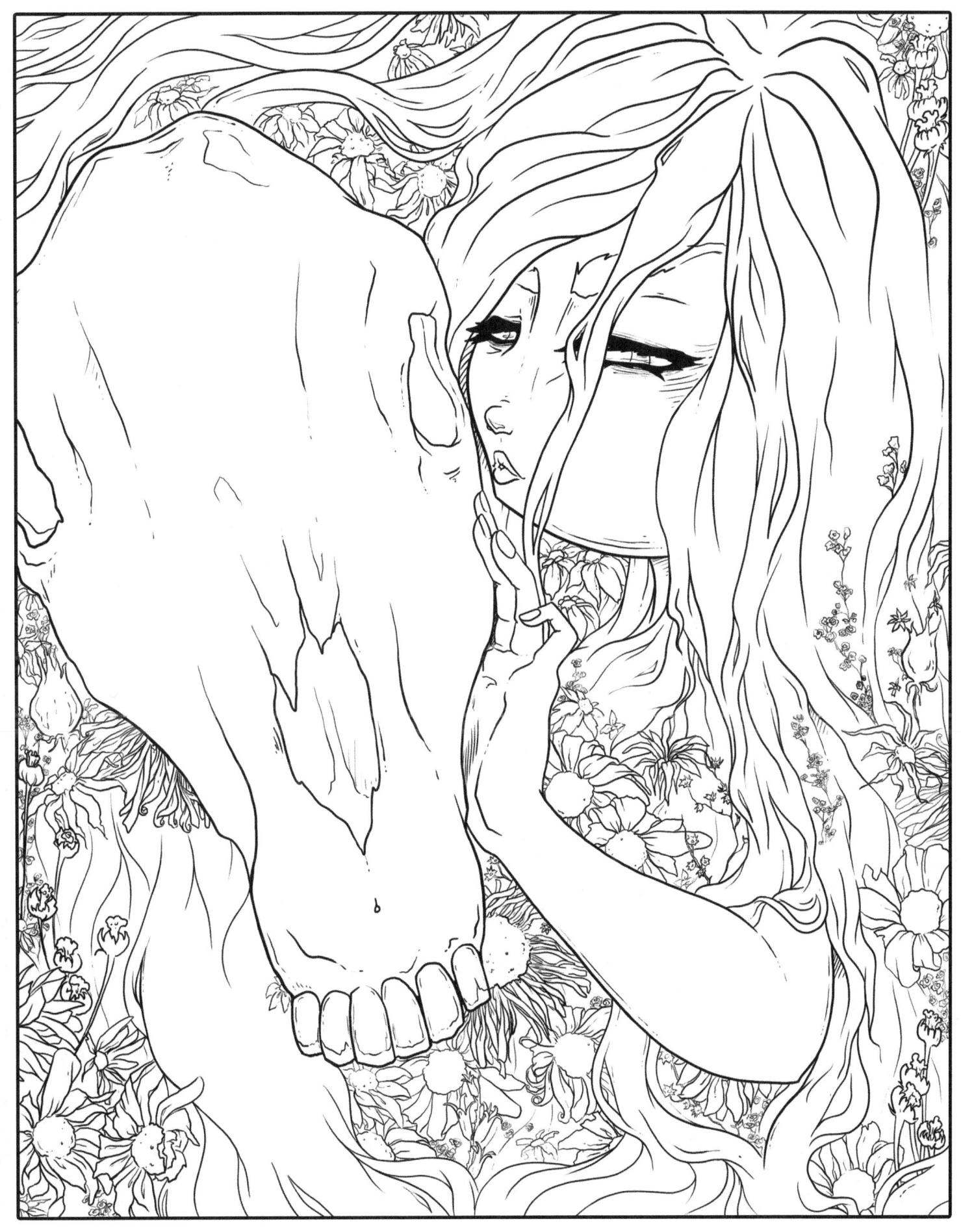

© 2017 Misfits Vol. 9 - Gothic Fantasy - White Stag - WhiteStagArt.com   Midsummer Night's Dreary

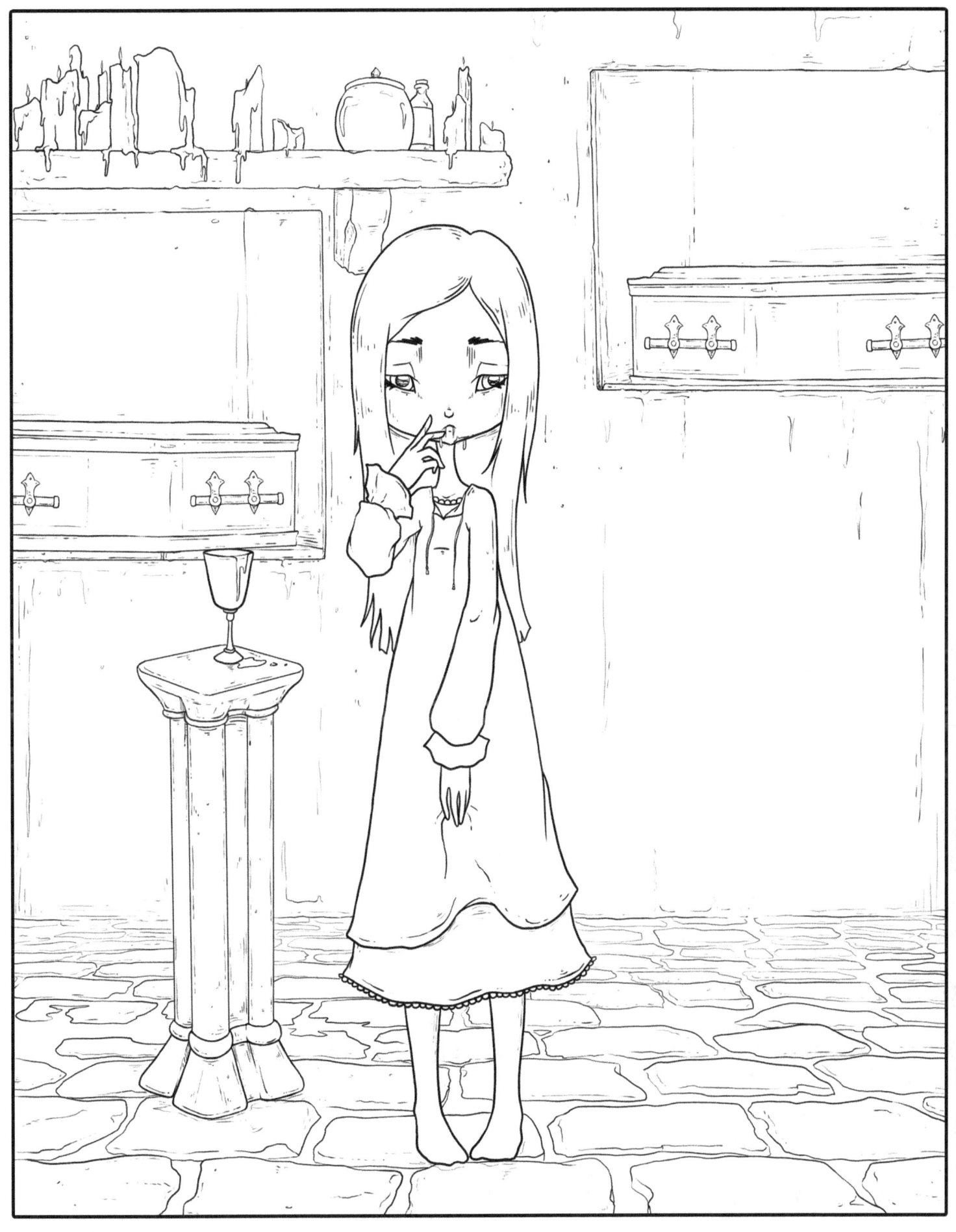

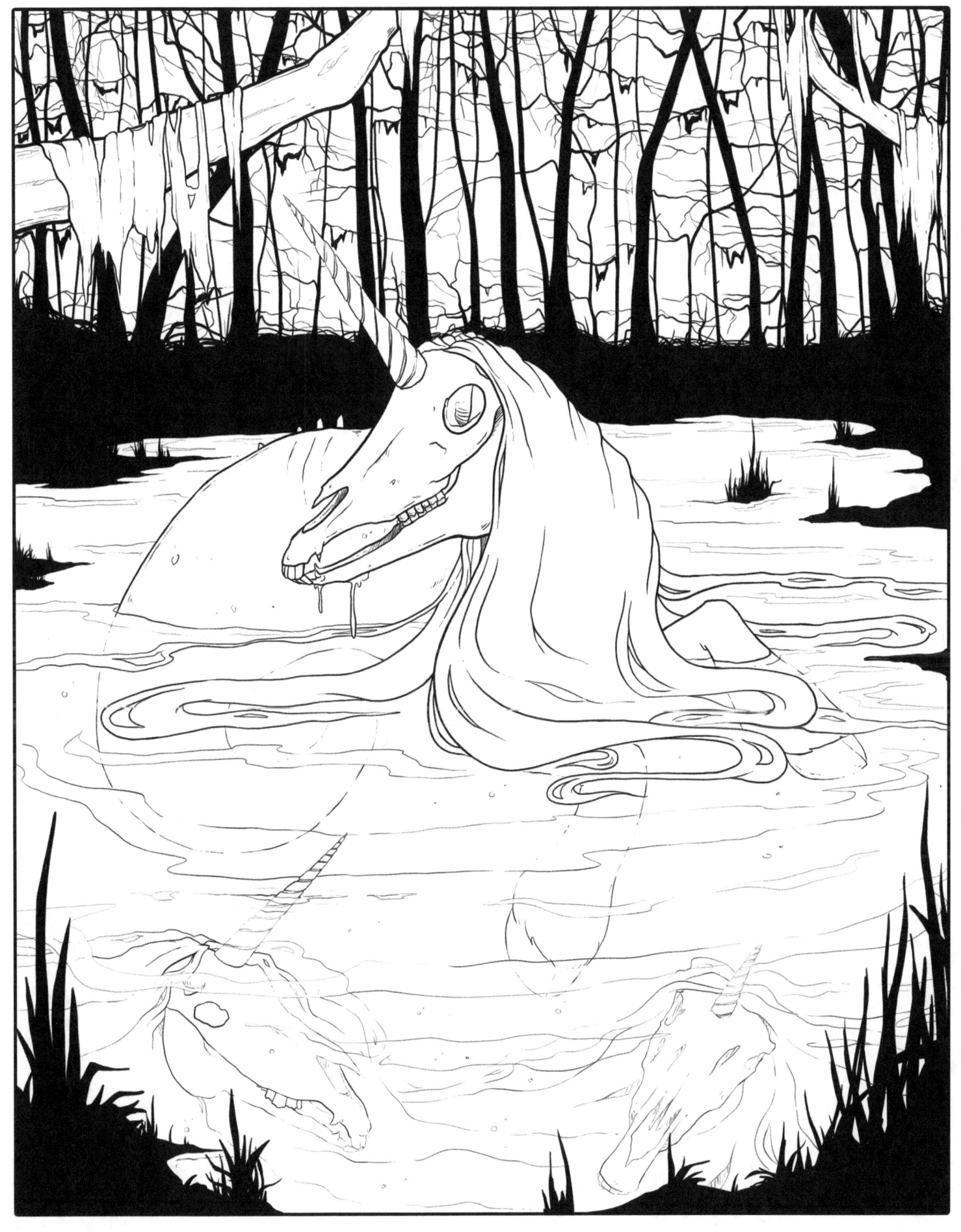

Free Kelpie Rides

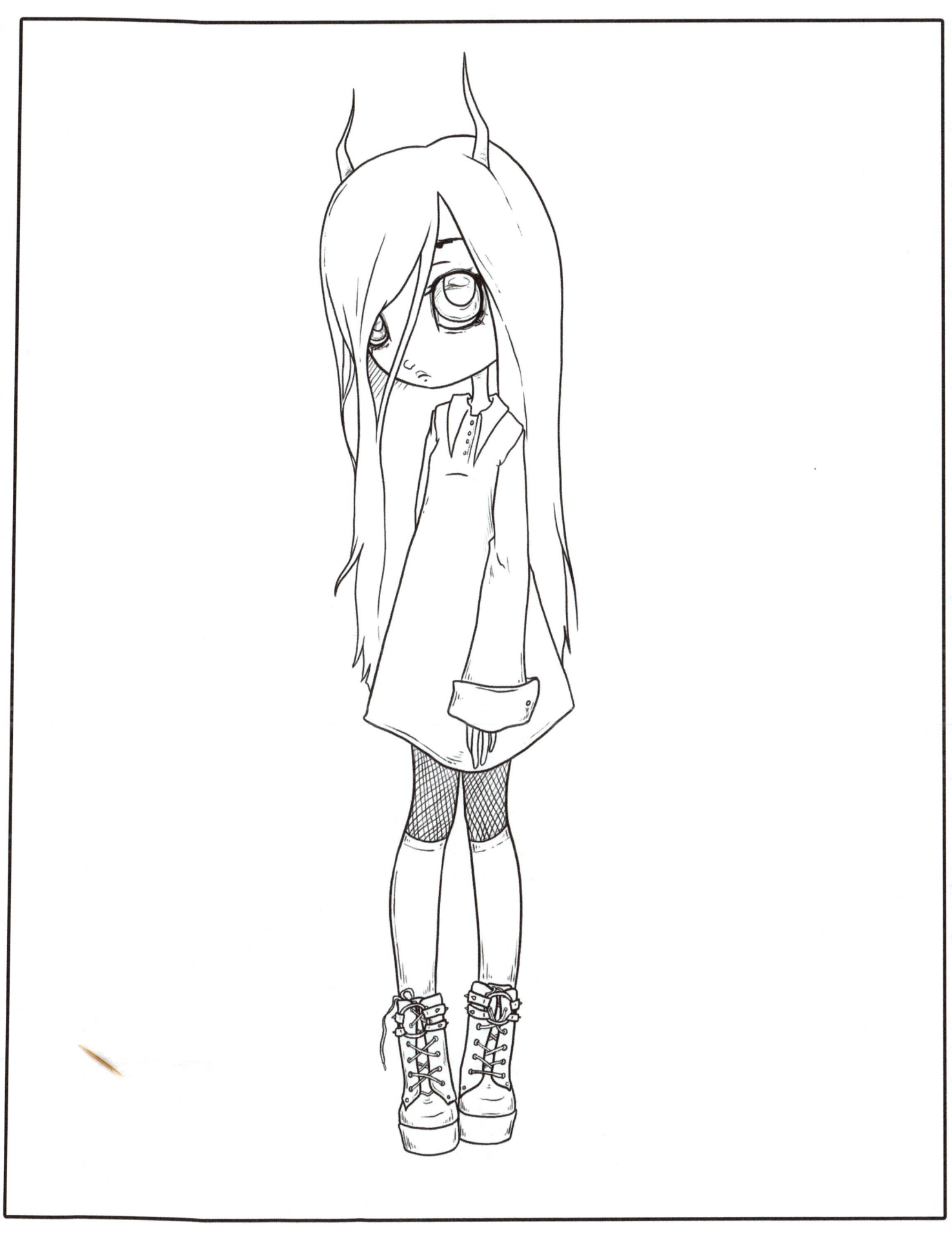

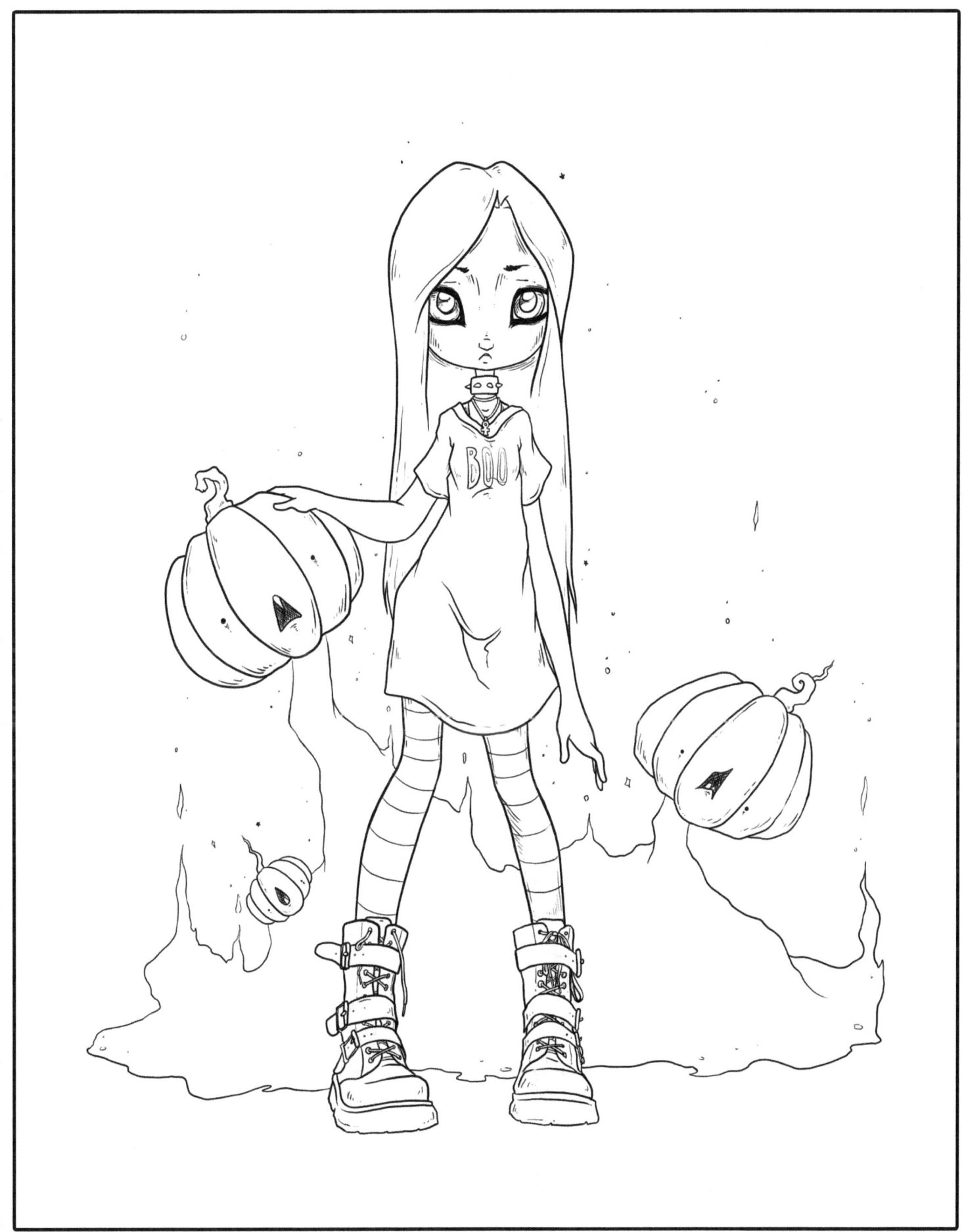

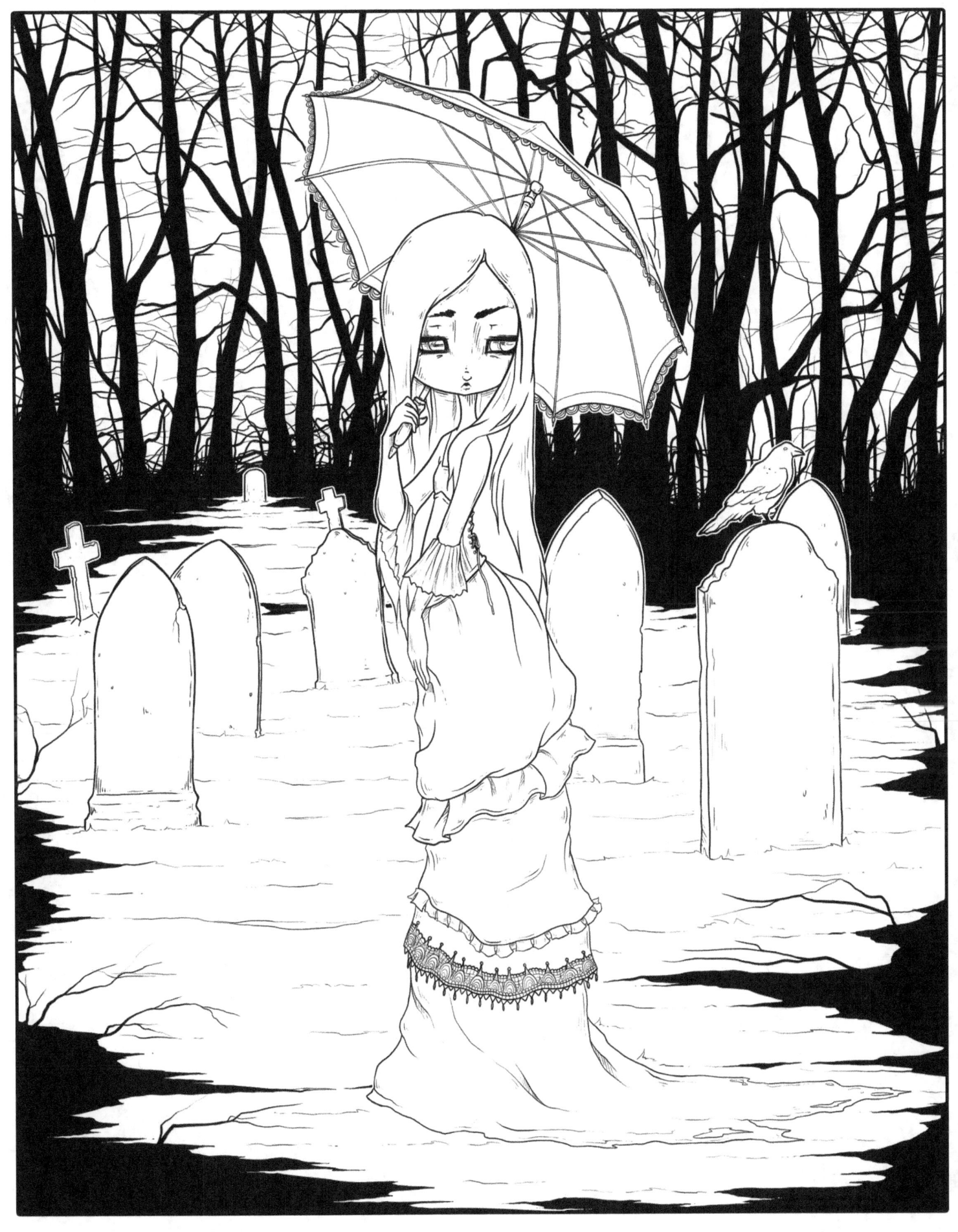

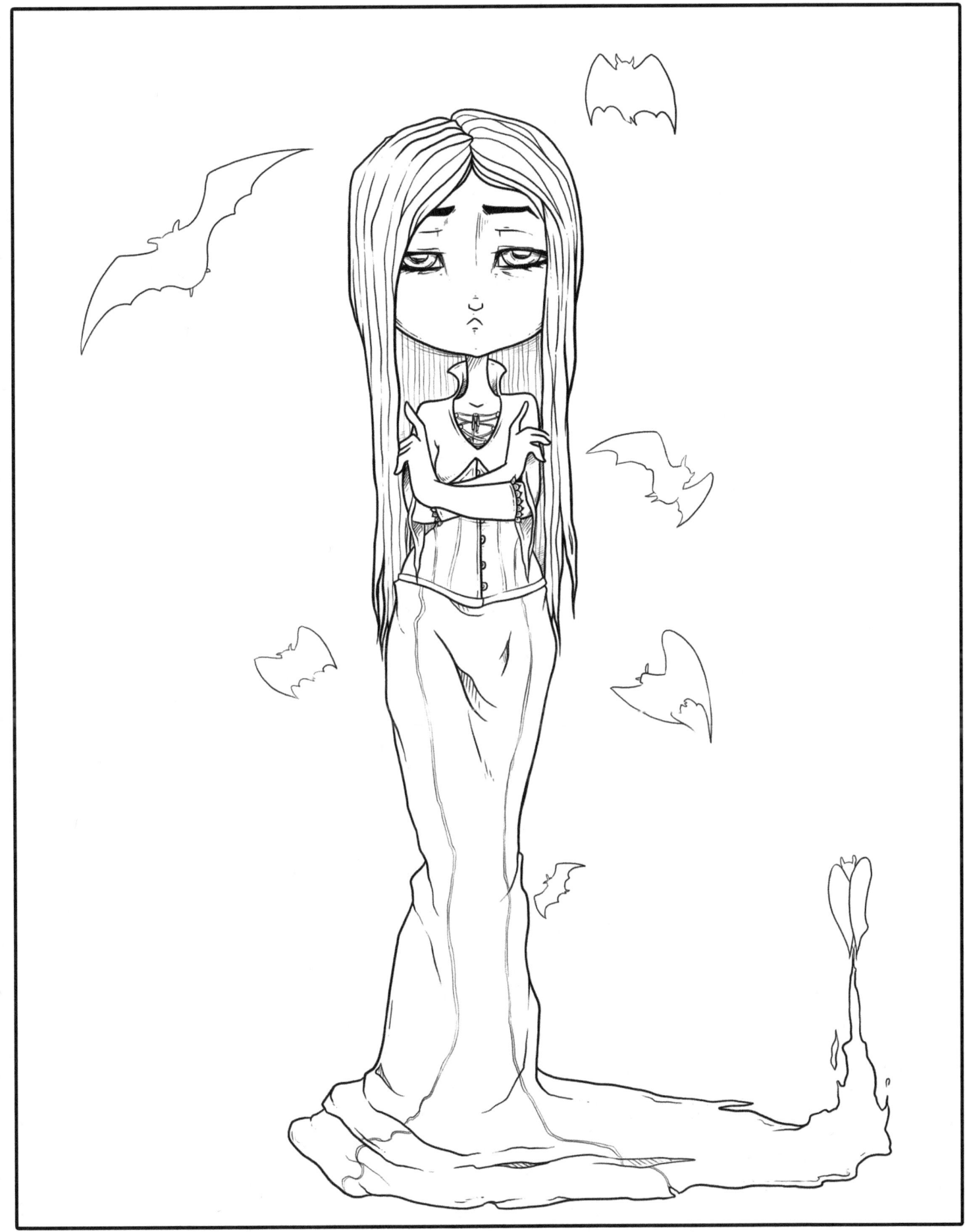

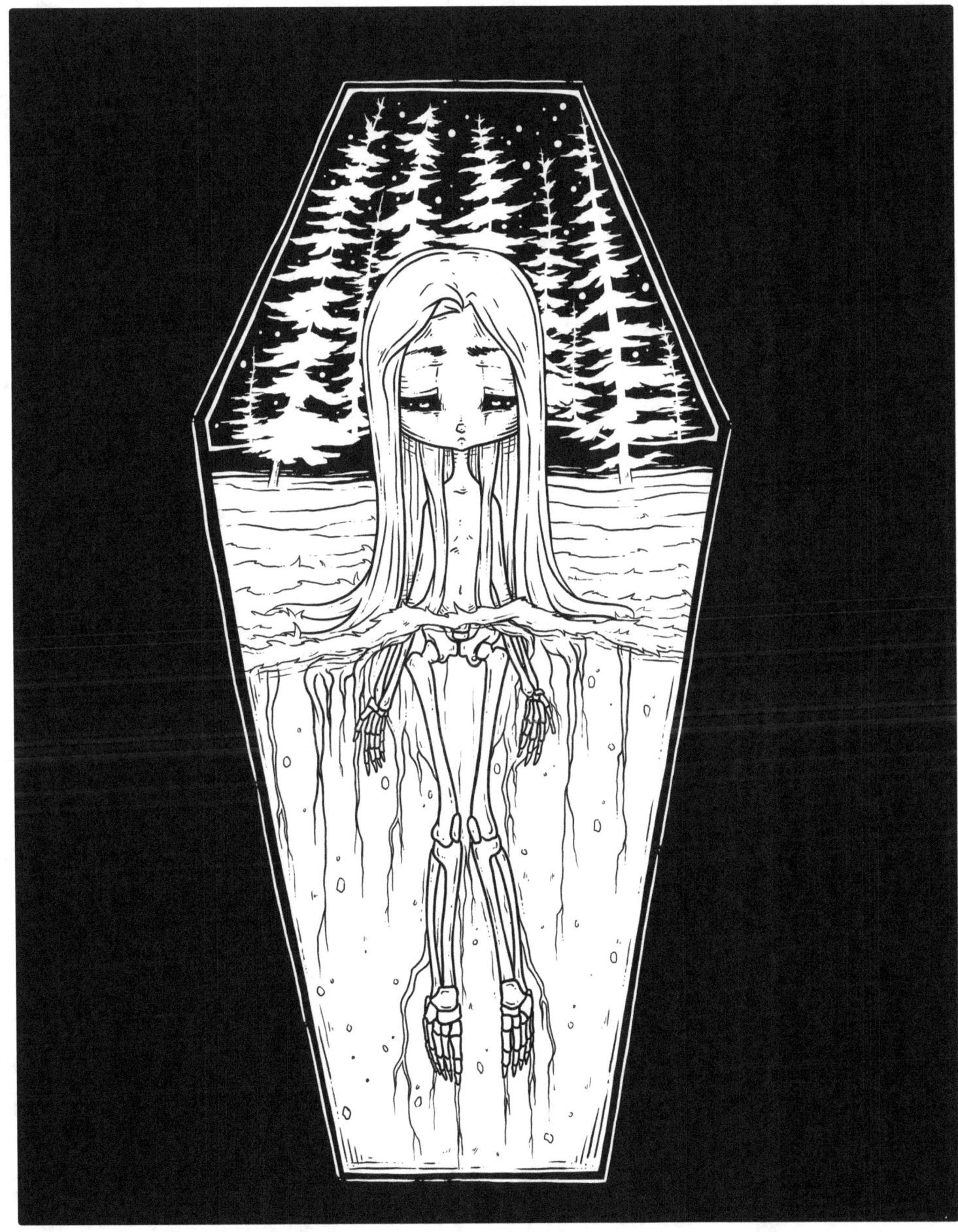

© 2017 Misfits Vol. 9 - Gothic Fantasy - White Stag - WhiteStagArt.com   BECOME

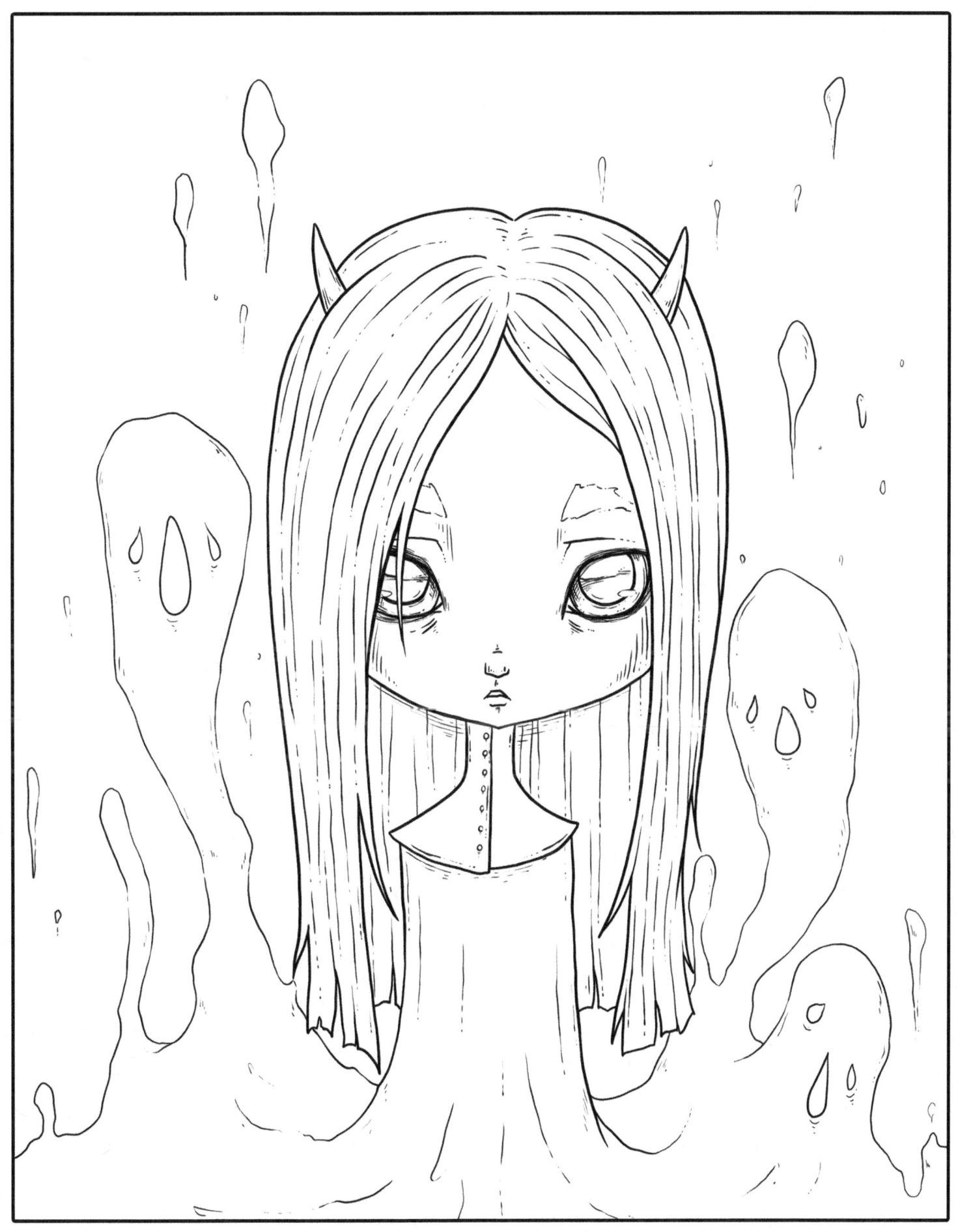

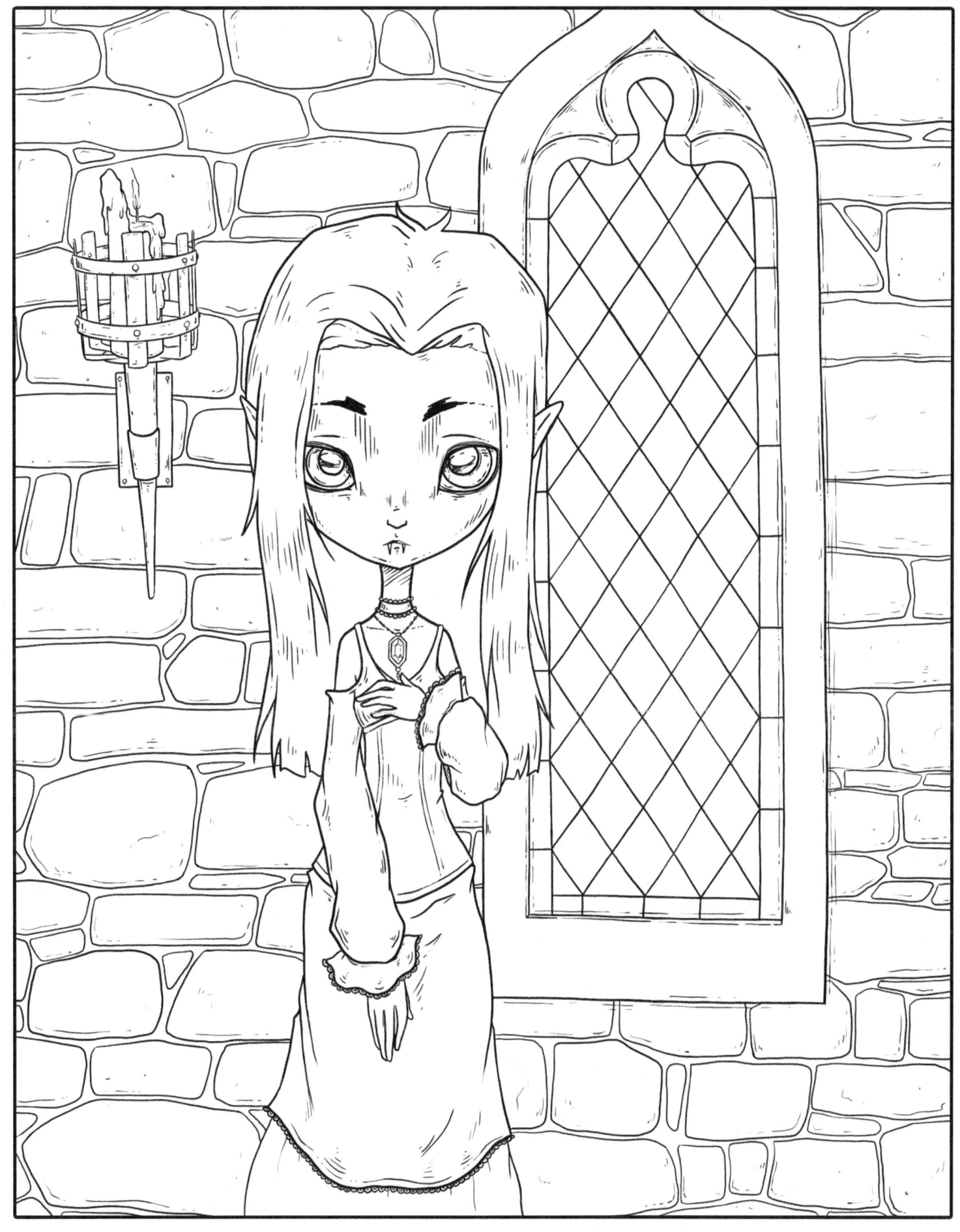

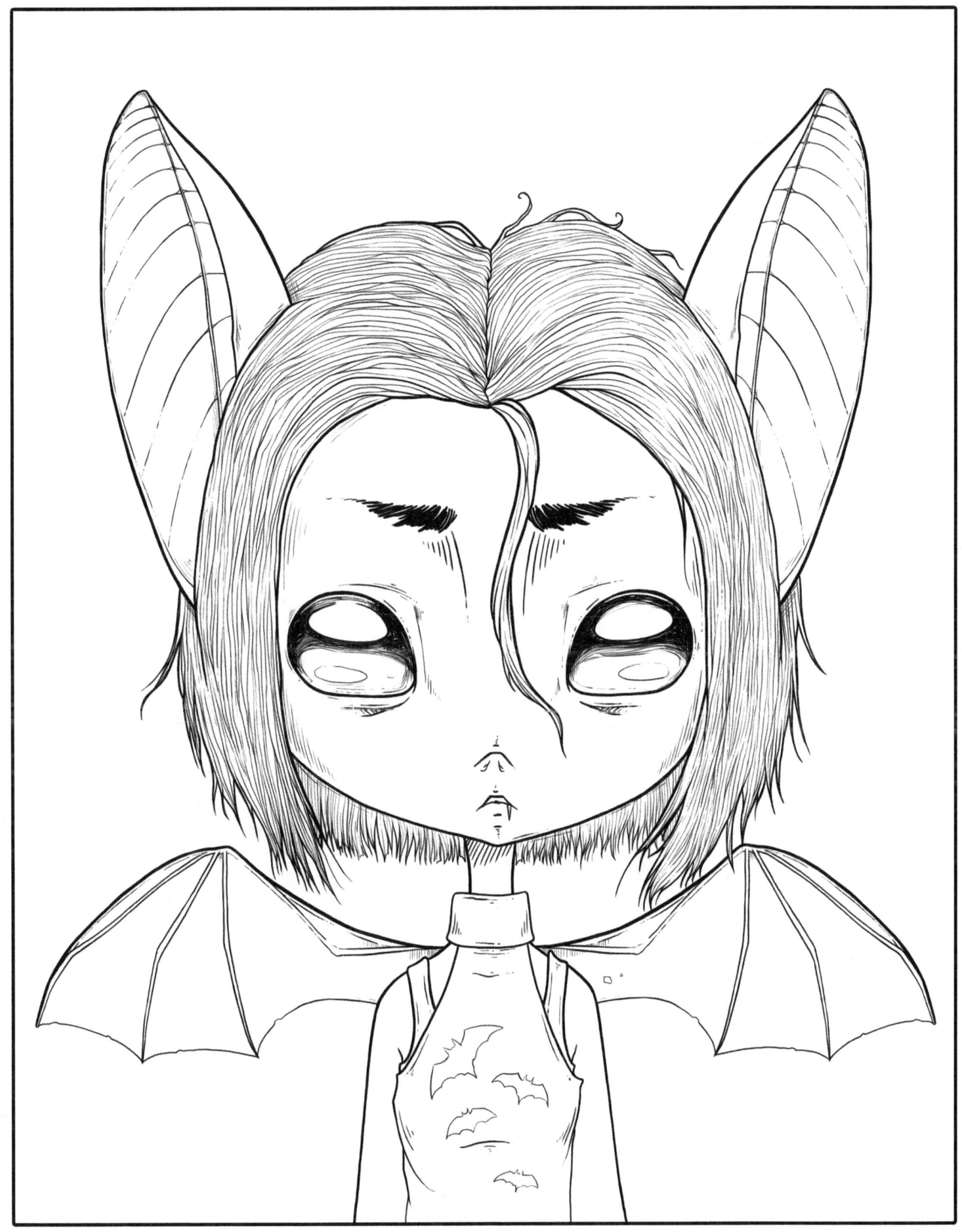

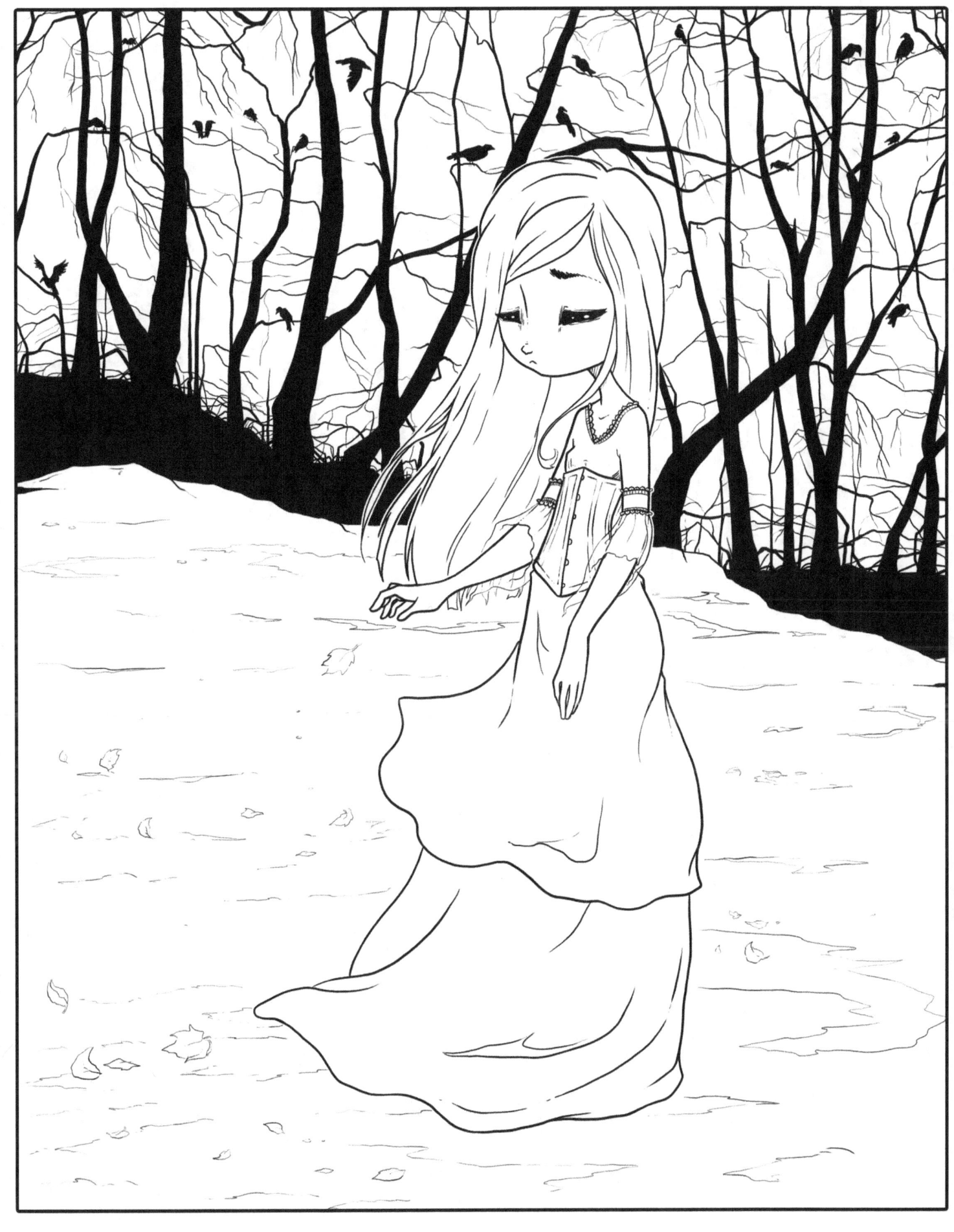

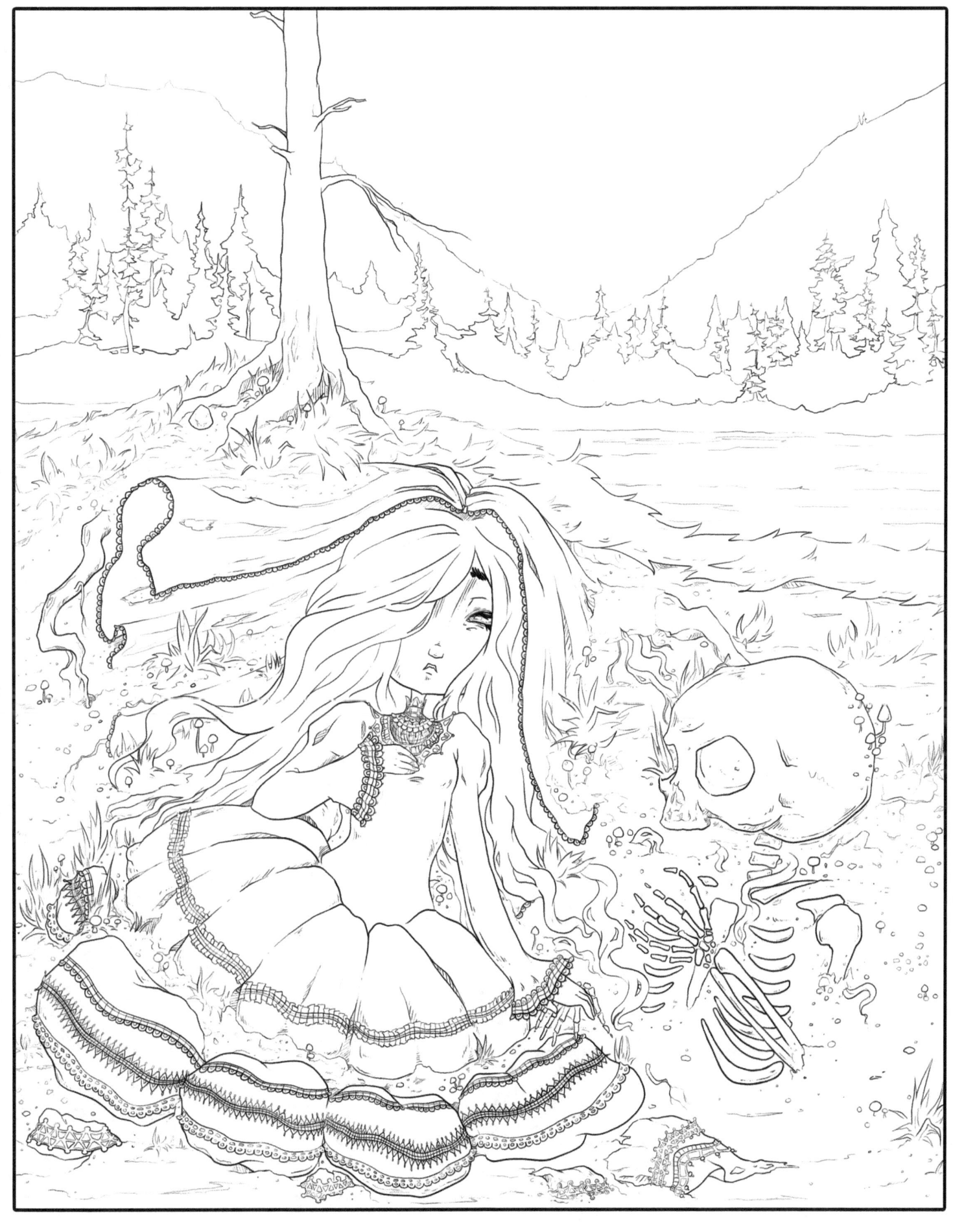

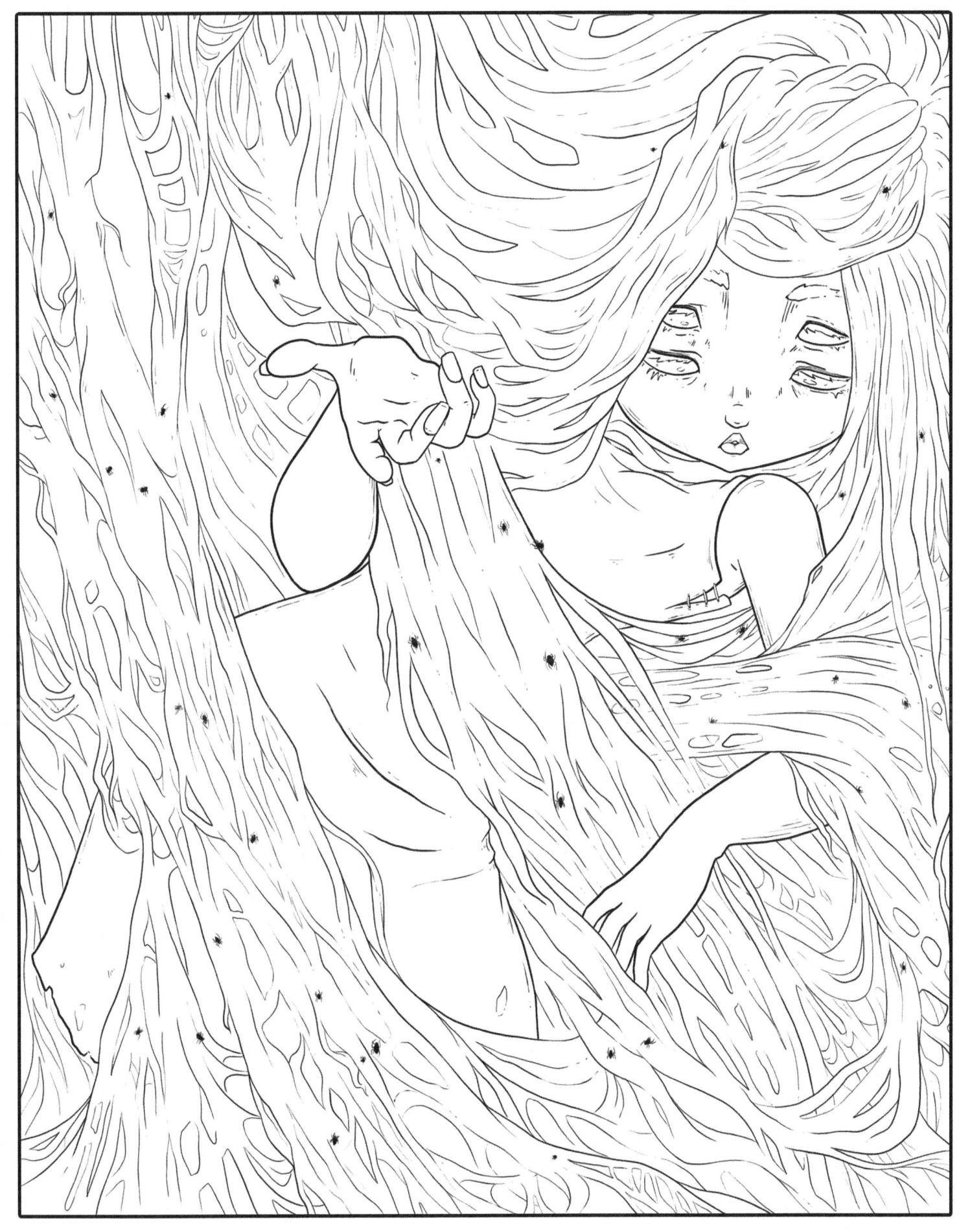

© 2017 Misfits Vol. 9 - Gothic Fantasy - White Stag - WhiteStagArt.com   In Her Hair...

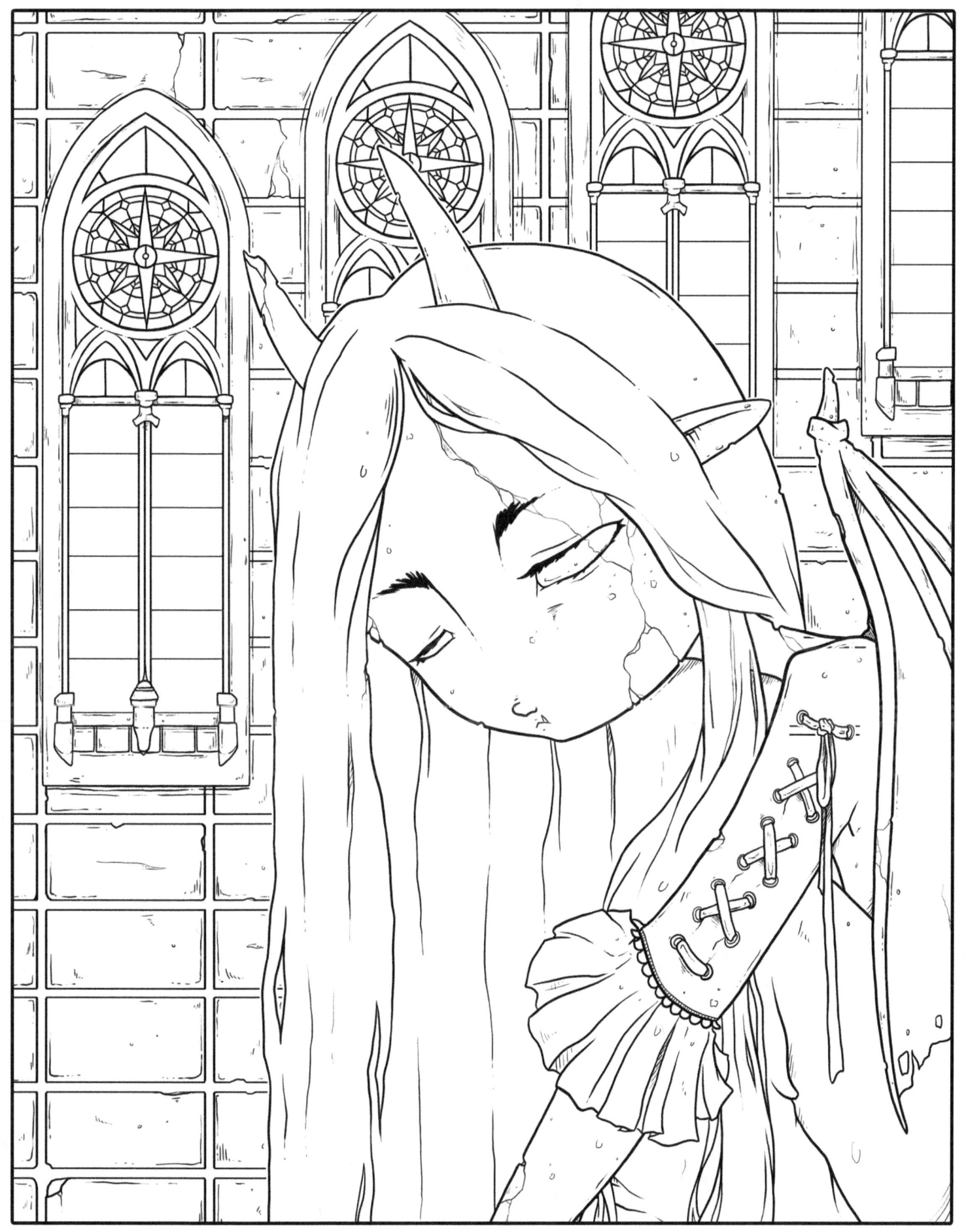

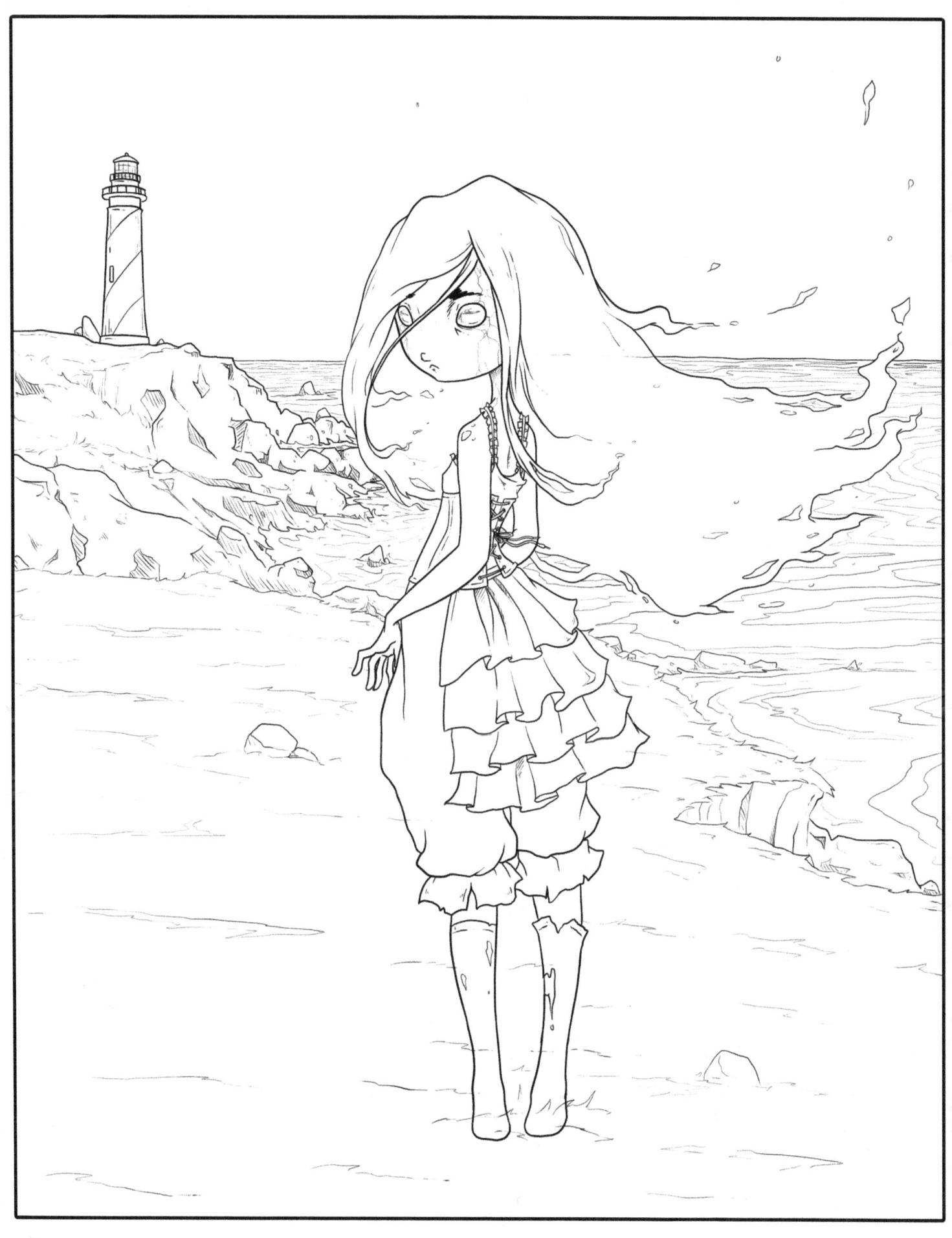

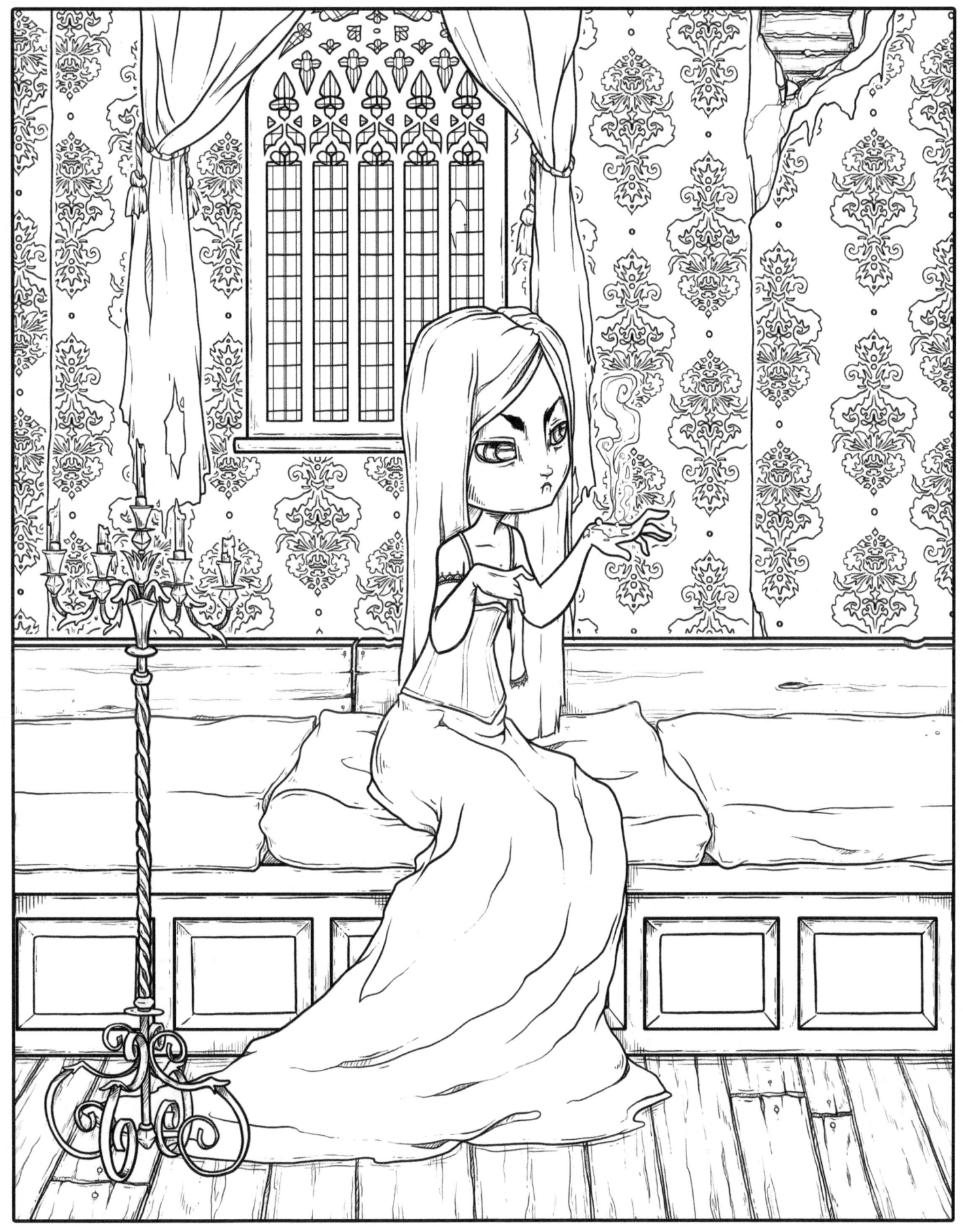
© 2017 Misfits Vol. 9 - Gothic Fantasy - White Stag - WhiteStagArt.com   Close the Curtains...

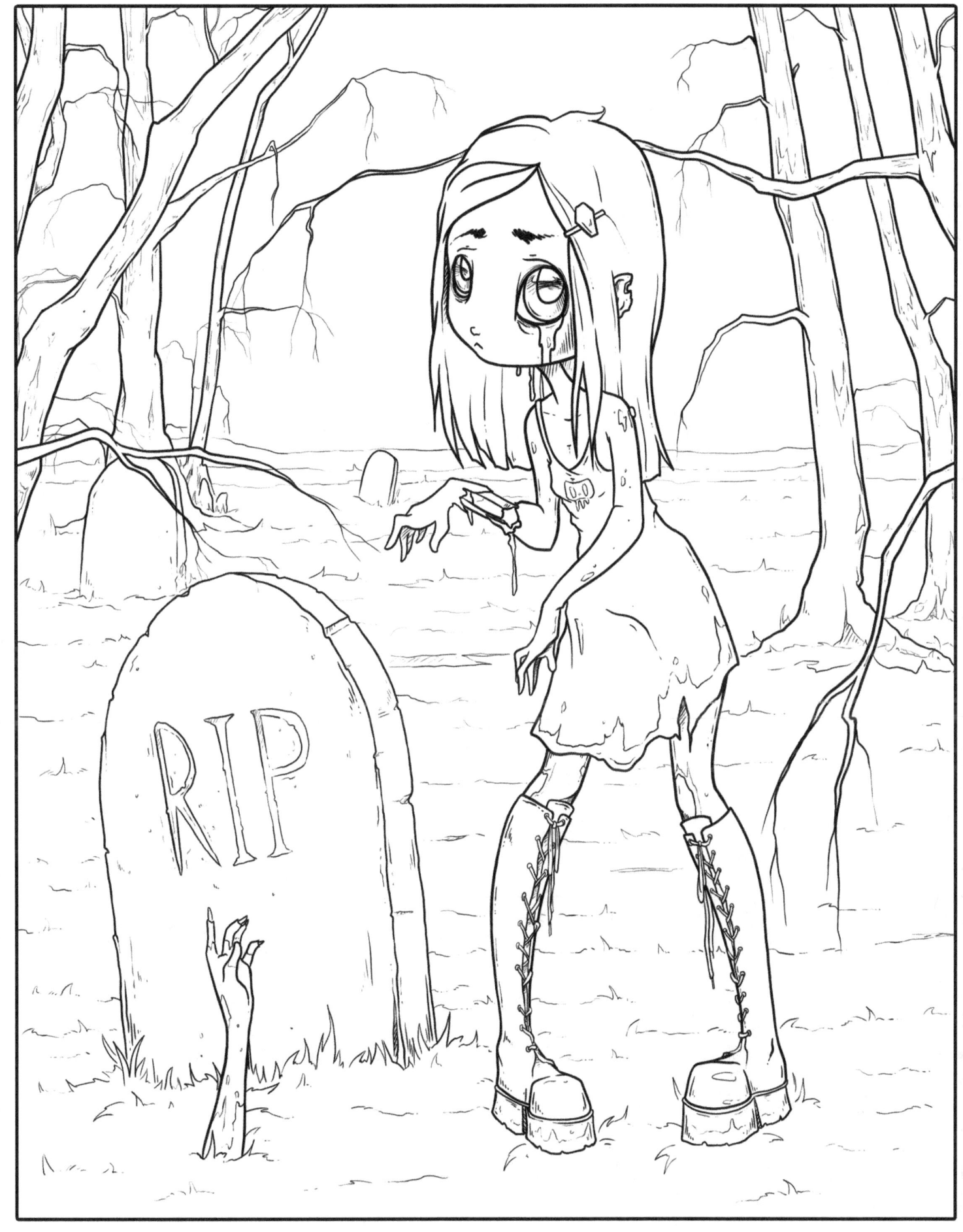

© 2017 Misfits Vol. 9 - Gothic Fantasy - White Stag - WhiteStagArt.com   **Rise**

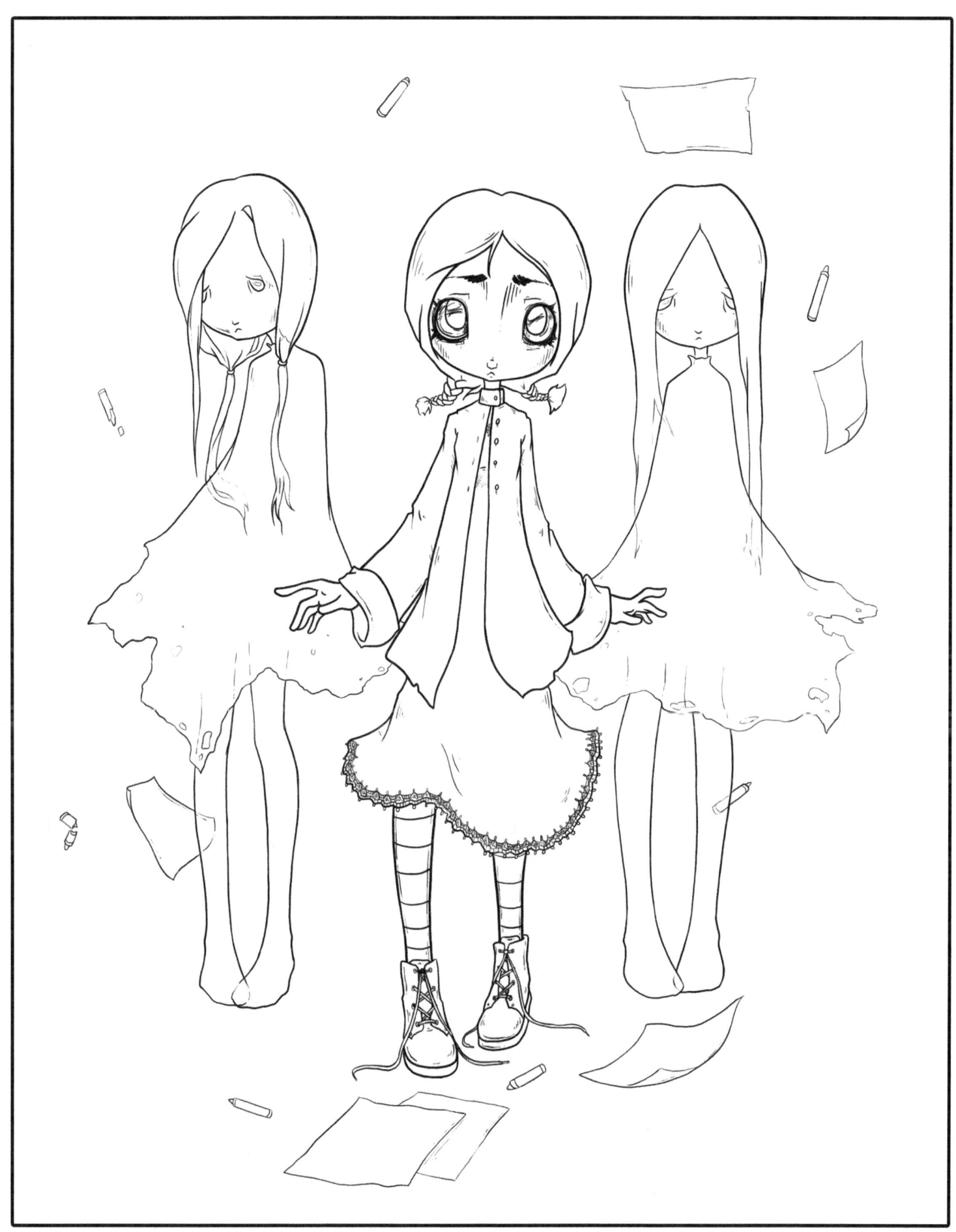

© 2017 Misfits Vol. 9 - Gothic Fantasy - White Stag - WhiteStagArt.com When all my Friends are Dead.

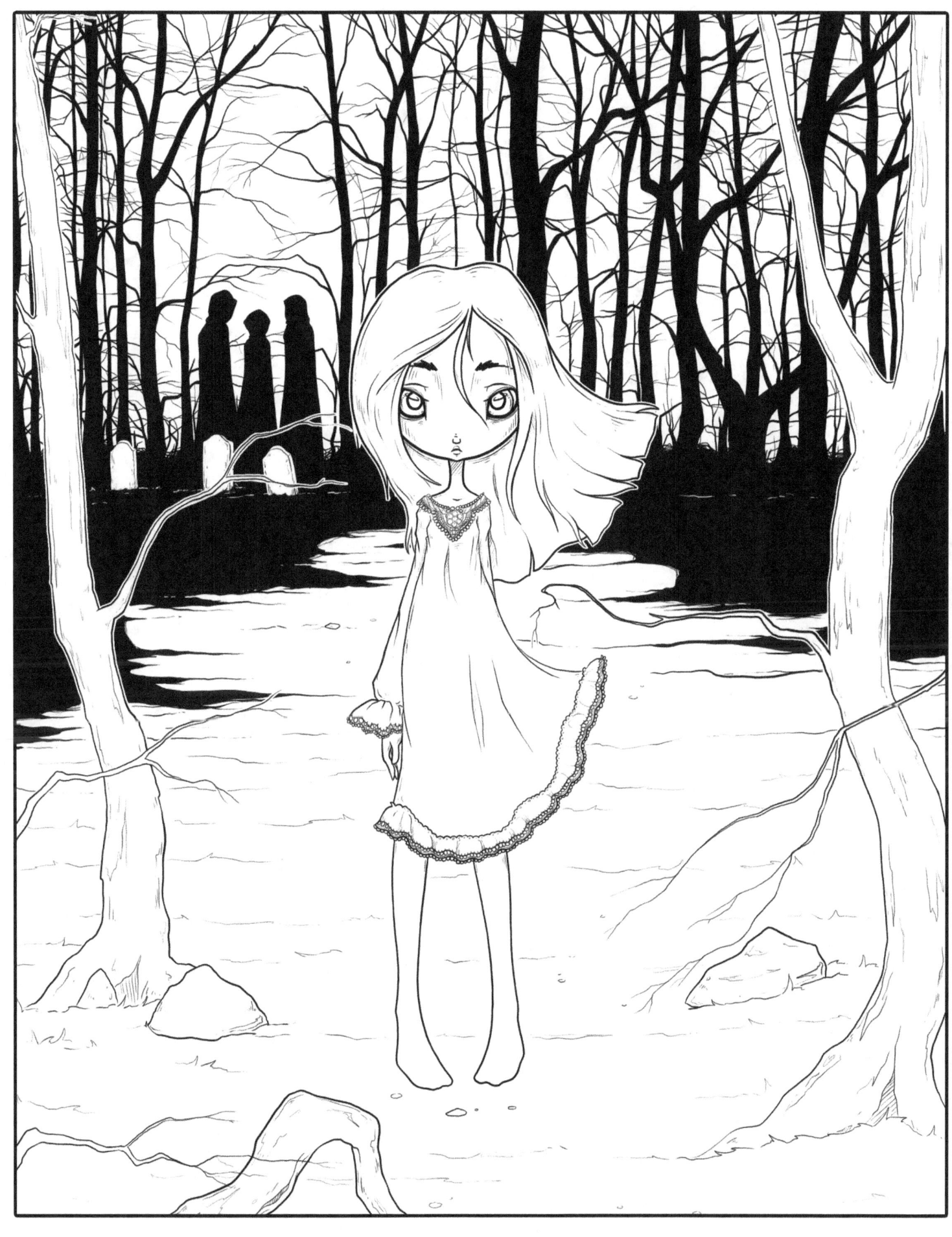
Friends in the Woods.

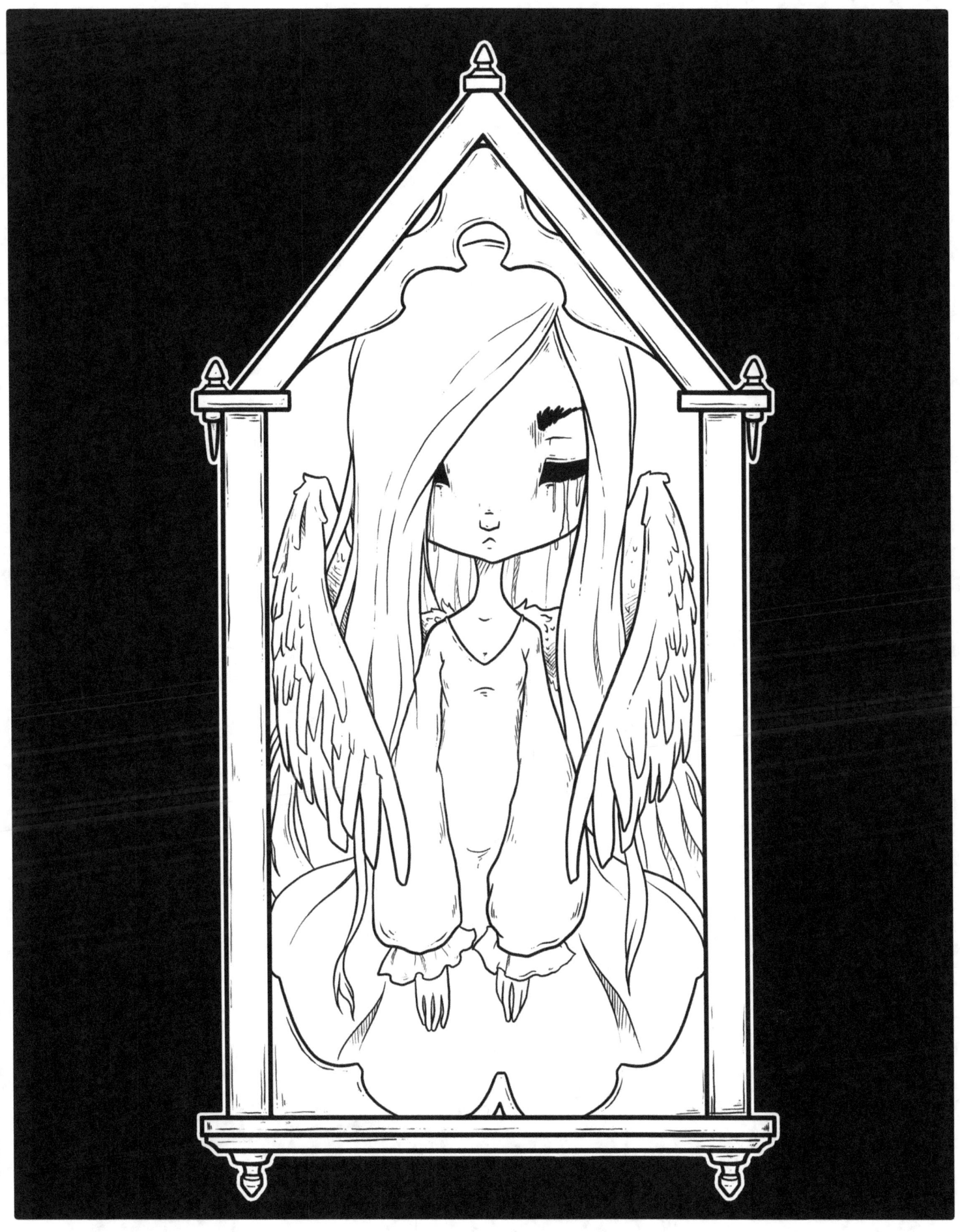

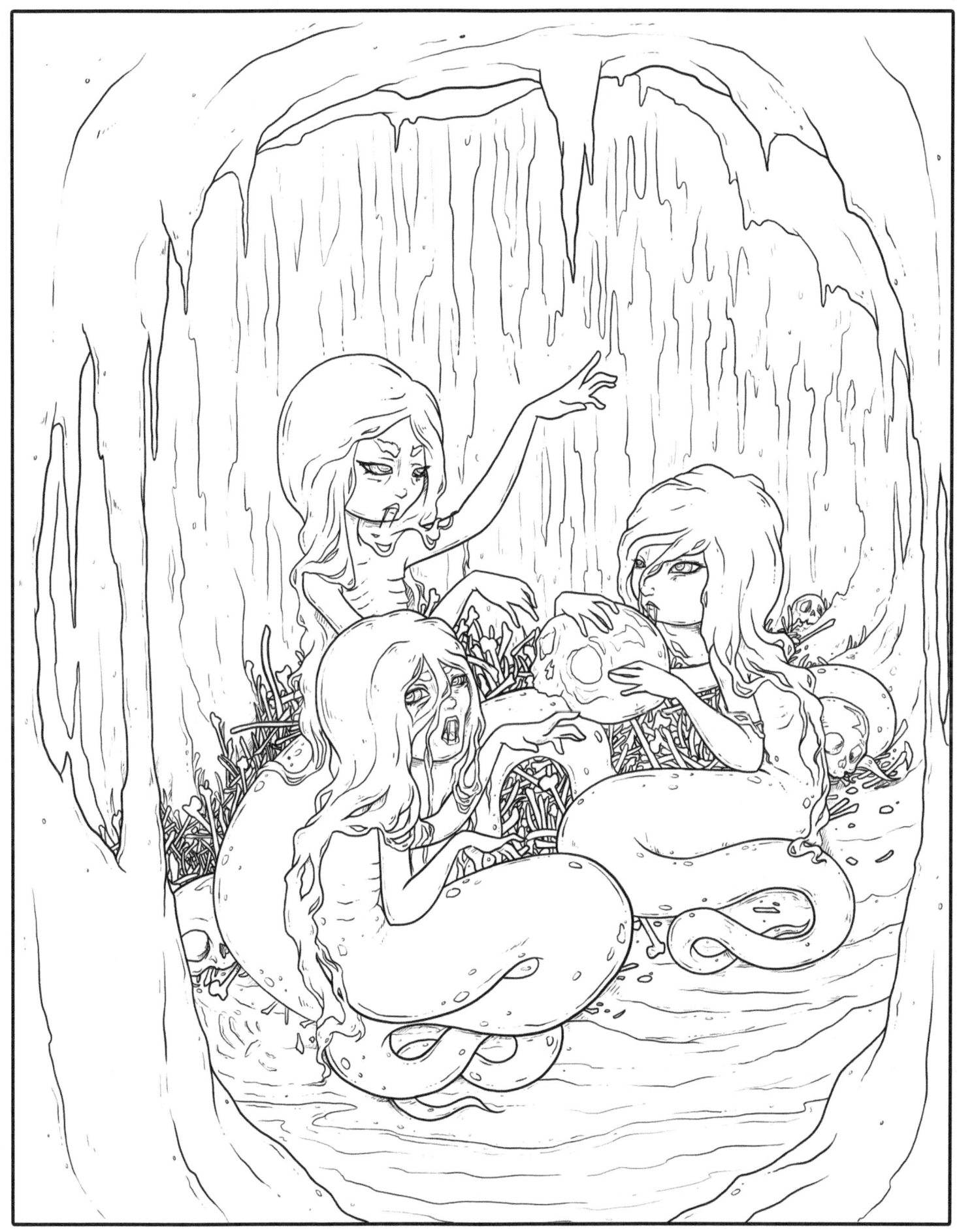

The Lair

White Stag.

This volume contains 25 brand new images filled with concepts for potentional future paintings and a couple from paintings I have done. This books to me has been the most inspiring to work on to date and so far the most complex based on themes... I hope you all have enjoyed it and have a very merry Halloween! I would love to thank everyone for the support so far and together with your input we can make each book better then the last!

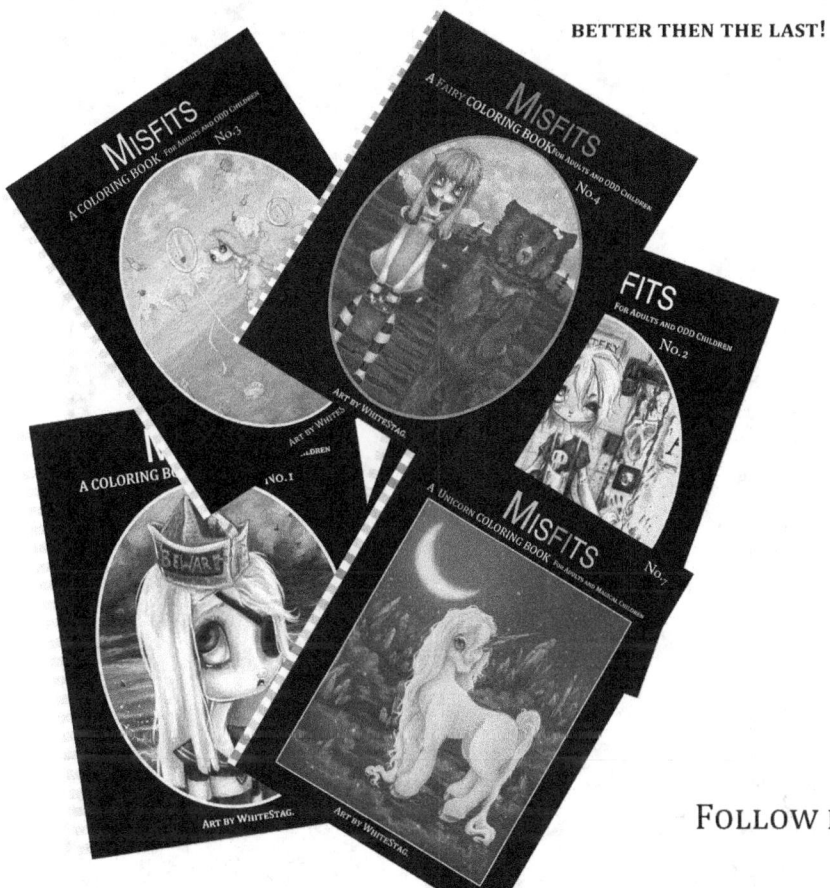

More Volumes Coming Soon!

Cryptids
Yeti! -A mini book
Fairy Creeps
More Zombies
Mermaids
+ more mini misfits

On Amazon Now!

Voulume 1- Medley of my art
Voulume 2- Zombies
Volume 3 - Another medley
Volume 4 - Fairies
Volume 5- Nautical
Volume 6 - Halloween
Volume 7- Unicorns
+Mystic Misfits (A Travel sized book)
Volume 8- Aliens

Follow me on Social media for previews and Releases.

I Love to see your finished images feel free to share your colored images on social media! Just Make sure to list the book you got it from.

Check out the New Facebook group for you to share your images to and chat with Stag!

www.facebook.com/groups/ODDchildren/

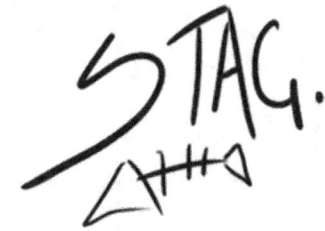

Prints, Paintings and More: www.LowbrowMisfits.com

| WhiteStagArt.com | facebook.com/TerraFantasyArt |
| Instagram.com/WhiteStagArt | Twitter.com/WhiteStagArt |

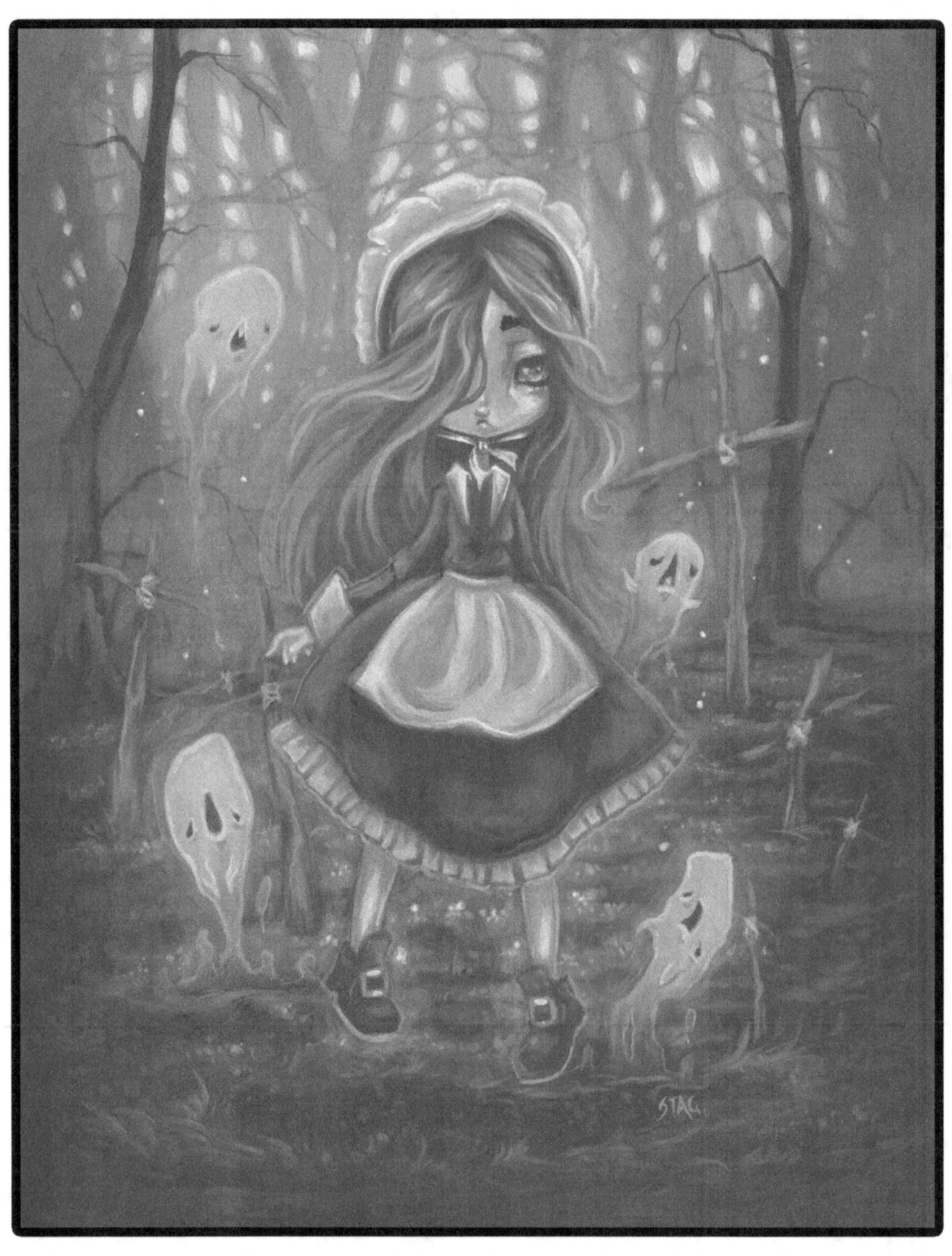

To Astel and Ansley.... May every day be Halloween.

www.ingramcontent.com/pod-product-compliance
Lightning Source LLC
Chambersburg PA
CBHW082220220526
45470CB00010B/3249